I0481311

The

Banking

Effect

Revised Version 2

ISBN-13: 978-1984132840
ISBN-10: 1984132849

Contact Information:

Dan Thompson

Wise Money Tools

www.wisemoneytools.com

208-939-5910

Email: danthompsonsdesk@gmail.com

Road To Wealth..7

4 pillars of freedom 11

Pillar 1 12

Pillar 2 13

Pillar 3 14

Pillar 4 15

Averages Lie 18

Taxes At Retirement...............................20

Opportunity Cost...................................21

How Does It Work?................................23

Where the "Safe" Money Is 25

The Magic Eye 27

What Type Works Best? 30

What Most People Don't Know 32

Saving or Investing?...............................32

The Long Life 36

Why an Insurance Company? 40

Dividends 42

Paid Up Additions.................................44

The Final Benefit 50

Real Life 53

Other Strategies 56

Biography 61

Foreword

Once again you will be introduced to ideas that you may have never heard of before, nor knew they existed. Why? I wish I had a good answer for that. The only thing that I can think of is "comfort." Not YOUR comfort, but the comfort of those from whom you seek financial advice.

These "Financial Advisors" get comfortable with their products, they may not be looking for better solutions, and worst of all they may not be able to even look "outside-the-box." And why is that? Because of who they work for, or who they are affiliated with. Yes, it's true; many financial firms dictate what products their advisors can promote and sell. Your advisor's hands might be tied. He/she may not be able to offer certain products to you. In addition (and this in my opinion is much worse), he/she may be "coerced" into selling you their specific products in which the company makes a greater profit!

Either way, be it out of comfort or control, an Advisor who cannot bring, embrace, or furnish his clients with some of these ideas and concepts may not only be hurting himself/herself and their future but ultimately you, the investor, looking for strategies and ideas that really work.

After reading this book you may find a lot of things that you thought were true about money, risk, and investing are not, the question is, once you have the knowledge, what will you do about it?

Road To Wealth

We all have a common goal when it comes to saving and investing.

What is it?

We are trying to acquire enough wealth to retire in some fashion.

Maybe retirement is the best word to use here, because retirement has a different meaning for everyone in terms of what they want to do and how they want to live, so let's define it as this:

"Having enough money to do what you want to do, when you want to do it, and that you don't run out of money before you run out of life."

I think most everyone I talk to would agree that that is the reason they save and invest.

In short, we'll call it "WEALTH."

The problem that I see comes from the financial planning firms and Wall street.

They don't have solutions or strategies to build wealth without the risk that goes along with it.

They call it the risk reward paradigm. They say you have to take greater risk to get a greater reward – or return.

In fact, the regulators would cringe if you even suggested that you could take little risk for a high reward.

I like to show this cartoon as an example — I want you to take a good look at it.

What do you see?

What this cartoon depicts you, as an investor, running down the middle of Wall Street.

You are dodging "market crashes," "interest rates," "inflation," "risk," and maybe the worst of all, "fees!"

That's just a few of the more obvious risks. Forget about other risks such as having income for life, longevity, timing, and Sequence of return risk.

That just puts more traffic in your way.

The objective, as we stated earlier, is to get to your goal of "wealth."

You're in traffic, putting your money at risk, trying to make your way through all the cars (risks) that could crush you.

You'd like to find a better and safer way; however, your broker/advisor/planner keeps telling you to stay in the traffic, it's the only way. You have to risk it all to get where you want to be.

Meanwhile, many wise investors, like Warren Buffet, Charlie Munger, Ray Dalio, Monsesh Pabrai, Guy Speirs, and others like them are on the sidewalk. Safely making their way towards Wealth.

In fact, they are moving along much faster than you, and with no risk.

And guess who else is on the sidewalk out of traffic?

It's the Wall Street executives and even your financial advisor.

You would be shocked to know how few mutual fund managers there are that have their own money in the fund.

That's right, they don't even put their own money at risk in the funds they manage.

See you take all the risk. Wall Street is happy to your fees and keep you thinking the only way to wealth is to fight your way through the traffic.

Even if you tried to get on the sidewalk, your financial advisor would push you into the street, telling you, you'll never make it on the sidewalk.

Don't listen to Buffet, he was just lucky.

By keeping you blinded and in the traffic, you keep paying their fees, while Wall Street safely builds their wealth on the sidewalk.

Sadly, this is the reality that most everyone who is reading this book faces.

I'm going to show you a better way. A safer way. A more predictable way.

A way to walk on the sidewalk towards your destination of wealth — AND GET OUT OF THE TRAFFIC!

4 pillars of freedom

My guess is you're about as frustrated as everyone else is out there about their money, investments, and retirement.

Ever wonder when you can comfortably retire?

Are you relying solely on the stock market for your wealth?

Is your money being "professionally" managed by a brokerage firm, an Investment Advisor, or a mutual fund?

So, how's that working out for you?

And how is your 401k? Worried it may not be enough or that the market could cut the value in half like in 2008?

If you're like most people, you might be a bit nervous.

You're not alone – sadly it's the state of affairs for most Americans these days.

High risk – low rewards – riding up and down with the tide – feeling completely out of control.

So what are you going to do when the next stock market crash comes – and oh, it's coming.

How many more times can you take a massive sell off and you're left holding the bag?

There is a better way, a much better way.

It's easier than you might think.

We are a bit backwards here in America; we tend to build our wealth by first taking excessive risk, then cross our fingers and hope for the best.

Well my friends, hope is NOT a strategy!

Let me talk to you about the 4 pillars to financial freedom.

Pillar 1

Be the master of your house – be debt free – owe no man!

This is one area where so many people struggle. Why? Because debt is so easy!

It all starts with school debt. Many college graduates were sold a bill of goods.

Get a loan, go to school and get an education and then and only then will you get your dream job!

Sadly, that doesn't happen for most graduates.

What's worse is not they are shackled with years and even decades of school loan payments.

And the government, in cahoots with the banks, have

assured that there is no way to ever be forgiven for the loan through any kind of discharge or bankruptcy – at least not for 25 years.

Can you think of anything safer for the banks?

Did you know that school loans and back taxes are the only debts you can never discharge? Even taxes can be negotiated in some cases, but not your school loan.

Once out of school, the next purchase is a car, then a home, and for the most part those are purchased with debt as well.

To make it even more difficult so many families live paycheck-to-paycheck and that means things like repairs, maintenance, vacations, and toys go on credit cards and additional loans.

It's vicious cycle that's not easy to get out of, but you have to!

Getting out of debt has to be priority.

Pillar 2

Put down your roots!

Have you ever thought how a tree survives a storm? Maybe you haven't thought about it consciously because you already intuitively know this,

But the only thing that keeps that tree from falling over

is the roots.

The deeper and stronger the roots the more punishment a tree can take from a storm.

Every one of us has what I call a wealth tree. Some are small some and just getting started and others are enormous.

Your wealth tree is either strong and growing, or susceptible to economic storms.

You need to have strong financial roots so that your wealth tree can withstand the economic storms that are sure to come.

This is your safe and accessible money.

No matter what economic storms come in, the root assets are what will keep your wealth afloat.

Those with deep roots are also the ones that walk on the sidewalks of life, laughing at you dodging the oncoming traffic.

Wouldn't it be nice to have some of your money, get out of the traffic?

Pillar 3

Capital is King!

I'm sure you know the golden rule when it comes to

money right?

"Whoever has the gold makes the rules!"

It's true, those with money, with capital, tend to make the rules, but more importantly get to take advantage of opportunities too.

Those with capital don't have to ask Mr. Banker for a loan when they need to make a major purchase either.

You can be your own private lender, your own bank. This can be a tremendous advantage over your lifetime.

So, capital truly is king.

The key is where to store your capital, how to access it when opportunities come along, and how to continually add to your capital base.

Finally, the 4th pillar I call it wealth squared.

Pillar 4

Wealth Squared

Once you have your roots,

Once you've amassed plenty of capital

It's now time to take advantage of exceptional situations to grow your wealth – squared!

What that means is having the same dollar, do two

things for you, that's why we call it wealth squared.

Look, most of us have been victims of the stock market and of money managers and mutual funds who said they can beat the market.

Didn't work out too well did it?

Money managers for the most part, at least those that the ordinary investor has access to, rarely beat the market, and certainly not consistently.

In fact, statistically they underperform the market – significantly.

Add in their fees and you're lucky to get a return at all in some cases.

The great investors – like Warren Buffet and Charlie Munger – do one thing that most investors don't.

They wait.

They wait and wait and sometimes they wait some more until the business or opportunity they are interested in goes on sale.

They often refer to it as an "event."

They have capital. When the price hits their target then they jump in.

The same goes for real estate, gold, oil, or even buying a business.

Charlie Munger has said, you don't make money on the buy or the sell, you make it on the wait – getting in at the right price.

But you'll never be able to take advantage of an opportunity unless you have capital

What does Wall Street and financial advisors teach? They want you to be invested 24/7 – 365.

So, in the 4th pillar is about keeping your powder dry, being patient, while still having your wealth grow and compound in a safe and tax advantaged account.

This is how you walk on the sidewalks, you don't dodge Wall Street traffic, you take safe and predictable steps towards building wealth.

Averages Lie

One of the greatest illusions that Wall Street and financial advisors use is *averages*.

Average returns DO NOT equal *Actual Returns*!

This is an important concept and must be understood or you'll likely be a victim to the false hope of averages.

Let's look at three different scenarios below. Each one of these has an average 5% rate of return.

However, depending on the severity of the ups and downs of the market, each statement has a different result:

Scenario 1	
Year 1	+15%
Year 2	-10%
Year 3	+10%
Average:	5%
Real Return:	4.41%

Scenario 2	
Year 1	+25%
Year 2	-15%
Year 3	+3%
Average:	5%
Real Return:	3.71%

Scenario 3	
Year 1	+30%
Year 2	-25%
Year 3	+10%
Average:	5%
Real Return:	2.31%

As you can see, they all averaged 5%. This is what your financial advisor will tell you.

You assume you can simply add 5% per year over the 3 years and that will be your new balance. However, you would be wrong.

Notice how the losses in the market have a greater impact on wealth than the positive of the gains?

The stock market from 1900 through December 2008, averaged 7%. However, its *real return* is 4.6%! That is a big difference isn't it?

Now calculate the taxes and fees on the overall return and where are you? It's pretty dismal, especially for all the risk you take.

Dalbar is an analytics company.

What Dalbar does is analyze investor behavior and the results of that behavior.

The last report from Dalbar ending December 2015 was really interesting when it comes to mutual fund investing.

Here are the results using an Asset Allocation fund:

10 years: 1.89%

20 years: 2.11%

30 years: 1.65%

Wow, are those the returns they told you that you would get when you first invested?

My guess is they said you would get 10% or 12% if you

held on long enough.

Well is 30 years long enough?

Oh, by the way, you still get to pay taxes on the growth as well.

Taxes At Retirement

The conventional thinking is that when you retire you will need about two-thirds of what you were making when employed. The idea being you will have fewer expenses and be in a lower tax bracket.

I recently heard a very interesting story by a man talking about his father.

He said, he came across a tax return of his fathers from 1960.

In 1960, the tax brackets neared 80%. However, you could deduct just about everything you bought. After all his deductions, his marginal tax bracket ended up at 12%.

Twenty-five years later he retired. He in fact, retired on two-thirds of his income. But now his tax bracket was **28%**. With little or no deductions, he had very little wiggle room. This is not just a 16% increase in tax rates. This equates to a **133%**

increase in his tax table.

This man's tax bracket actually increased during retirement and now he has really no way of reducing his income. The reason is that the majority of his income is coming from his retirement plan. In reality, he would have been better off paying his taxes at 12% or even 20% back while he was working and then placed his money in an account where it would never be taxed again.

Opportunity Cost

Let's take a minute and discuss Opportunity Cost.

Let me ask you this: Suppose I was to offer you stock in a company that today sells for $40 per share. In addition, I guarantee you that in 5 years, it will be worth $20 per share. How many shares would you like to purchase? Hopefully you said NONE!

This is exactly what we are doing when we pay cash for a depreciating asset such as a vehicle. Assume we are considering a cash purchase for a $40,000 car.

We are essentially putting $40,000 into a vehicle that is pretty much guaranteed to be worth half, or less, in 5 years. In other words, our $40,000 is going to dwindle down to $20,000.

When we pay cash for an item we give up the

"opportunity" for that money to work for us and grow….forever!

In our example, we are giving up the opportunity for growth on $40,000 that we used to purchase the car for cash.

Look at the various interest rates and years illustrated below. The chart shows what $40,000 could have grown

Years	5%	7%	10%	12%
5	$51,051	$56,102	$64,420	$70,493
10	$65,155	$78.686	$103,794	$124,233
20	$106,131	$154,787	$269,100	$385,851
30	$172,877	$304,490	$697,976	$1.4 Million

to in the future had I not used cash for my purchases:

Let's say I could get a safe and reasonable 5% rate of return. Twenty years from now, that car cost me in "opportunity" over $106,000. If I can make 7% on my cash, that could equate to over $154,000.

That amount of money might make a difference in someone's standard of living during retirement.

The result is that paying cash may seem like a great alternative to financing, which it does, but is it the best way to make a purchase.

How Does It Work?

Now let's talk about creating your own Private Banking System. This is a paradigm shift from where most of us are in our financial minds. It's a concept that has been around for 200 years, but seldom discussed by advisors as a means of generating wealth, mostly because even they do not know or understand the impact it can have on your wealth.

The concept is pretty simple. Rather than spend cash on a depreciating asset and lose opportunity cost as previously discussed, you save the capital in a private banking system.

When you need to make a purchase, you borrow from your private banking system. The important thing is that you must treat this loan as if the money was borrowed from a lending institution such as the corner bank.

It is extremely important that you are an "honest banker" and that you don't steal from your bank. In other words when you take a loan, you must repay the loan. Treat yourself as well as you would treat any other lender. Using funds with this method will assure that you replenish the principal used as well as the interest normally paid to other lenders. It's now all back in YOUR bank.

In order to make all of this work, we must first capitalize the private banking system. Similar to getting a bank charter, a newly established bank needs to have capital reserves in order to make loans.

Our private banking system is no different. We need to have capital in order to make loans. We have to save, transfer in, or invest capital into our private banking system. This can be rather quick, or may take some time, depending on your current income and asset availability.

Where the "Safe" Money Is

The IRS calls this vehicle an **IRC-7702**. The problem is that very seldom is this vehicle sold properly, particularly for banking purposes.

What is this vehicle? It is a maximized and over-funded *Permanent Life Insurance Policy*.

The same place banks put billions of dollars.

In my son, Jake Thompson's book "Money, Wealth, and Life Insurance he talks about BOLI (Bank Owned Life Insurance).

The FDIC makes available the balance sheets of nearly every major bank. The following figures are directly from FDIC.gov and represent the exact amount of money the following banks hold in life insurance.

Bank of America:	*$19,607,000,000*
Wells Fargo Bank:	*$17,739,000,000*
JPMorgan/Chase Bank:	*$10,327,000,000*
U.S. Bank:	*$5,451,892,000*

Banks are in the business of money. They have some of the most powerful people in the world, including economists, attorneys, accountants, financial analysts and other advisors, helping them increase the efficiency and use of their capital.

It is not insignificant that banks place billions of dollars in life insurance. It's a reflection of the value they place on this powerful asset.

For banks, it provides the ultimate in safety, stability, and growth. More importantly, the FDIC allows this asset to be classified as Tier 1 capital, which is the safest capital a bank can have.

Tier 1 capital is considered to be the core measure of a bank's financial strength.

We can learn a lot from banks, but they aren't the only ones benefiting from this powerful asset. Corporations are also heavily involved in buying life insurance in mass quantities.

It's not often we get the opportunity to do what the banks do with their money, and go directly to the source.

Banks take your deposits and buy billions in cash value life insurance. Now you can take your deposits and go directly to the insurance company yourself.

The Magic Eye

Did you ever see the books called "The Magic Eye?"

The Magic Eye books are filled with pictures that look like nothing more than a mass of psychedelic colors.

However, if you look closely, squint your eyes, and look cross-eyed, somehow a 3-D picture appears.

They made posters you could hang on your wall. The pictures were everywhere. I used to be fascinated with them and once you trained your eyes you could see the hidden pictures quickly.

High Cash Value Life Insurance and the Magic Eye pictures have a lot in common. As I met and worked with very wealthy clients, I began to see things more clearly.

Like those hidden pictures, it began to appear to me that the wealthier someone was, the more insurance played a part in their overall financial picture. The wealthy were not afraid to talk about insurance and position large dollars in a policy. It wasn't like those gurus on TV and the radio had proclaimed. The wealthy used insurance to their advantage.

I also noticed that as those who followed the "buy

term" mantra got older, they could no longer afford term coverage, and were usually forced out of their policy either by cost or health.

Statistically, only 1% - 2% of those who buy term insurance die with it intact.

Those who had the real wealth, used permanent insurance in some remarkable ways. Now I see it everywhere! Like the hidden pictures popping out at me, insurance can be quite a find. But I was stubborn and it took me a while to finally see it.

Nearly every wealthy person I know has incorporated life insurance as part of the overall plan for several reasons:

- It's tax friendly
- It's probate free
- It's the easiest asset to transfer at death
- Gives peace of mind
- Allows for greater charitable contributions with tax benefits – (we have an entire strategy devoted to this.)
- Has some of the highest and tax-free income streams of any safe money investments.

- Pays estate taxes with pennies on the dollar.

- Instantly provides for family left behind.

- It has tax advantages that no other investment does.

- Becomes a great retirement resource for families and business alike.

- Income from life insurance will not affect Social Security benefits.

- Works like your own private bank.

- Helps create a legacy to be passed on from generation to generation.

There are several items on this list that most people never knew nor were taught. In particular the banking concepts.

A policy that is correctly designed has more characteristics of a bank than it does an insurance policy. It is quite remarkable.

What Type Works Best?

For banking purposes, a mutual, dividend paying insurance company that issues a whole life policy has the characteristics best suited for banking.

As I said, these types of polices resemble a bank more so than an insurance policy.

Unfortunately, as with so many sound concepts there are those who take a concept and alter it and leave behind so many of the basic principles.

Currently, a couple of new players have emerged in the insurance world. They are called the "Indexed Universal Life" and the "Variable Universal Life."

I won't go into it in this book, but you want to run from any Universal Life Policy.

I have a 10 part video series on the IUL (indexed universal life) if you want an in-depth analysis of the danger those will be as people age.

You can see them at wisemoneytools.com

Those who try to tell you the UL makes for

wonderful "private banking systems" have not been educated enough. They are disasters in the making.

To put it succinctly, a universal life policy is built differently. The model it uses is flawed and will likely implode if you live a long life.

Don't let fictitious IUL and VUL illustrations sway you from a solid, predictable, proven method using dividend paying whole life.

Yes, it may be boring, but boring is exactly what you want when you are building wealth safely and securely.

It lets you walk on the sidewalk towards wealth, when you implement the strategies that Warren Buffet has taught for decades.

The objective is to not only live a long life and take advantage of the living benefits, but to die with a whole life policy too.

That may sound morbid, but it makes little sense to pay premiums into a policy for 15-20-30-40 years and then cancel it or have it lapse before you die and walk away from all of that money, talk about opportunity cost!

I'm not going to say much about the death benefit in your policy.

It's a bonus that will pay out immediately.

Your beneficiaries can then fund another banking system for their family and on and on, generation after generation.

What Most People Don't Know

Did you know that if you ever financed a purchase from a furniture store, car dealer, electronics, or a myriad of other items, most likely you were financed by an insurance company?

Many finance companies borrow blocks of money from insurance companies and then mark up the rate to their customers. They make money on the spread.

Most likely, if you've ever financed anything, you were paying – indirectly - into an insurance company. As the owner of a policy, you will likely be a lender to other financial institutions that borrow money from insurance companies for financing.

Saving or Investing?

Quick question, do you understand the difference between *saving* and *investing*?

I love the water. I'd pretty much rather be on or around water than almost anywhere else on the planet.

This past summer we had our daughter and granddaughter over to the house and as was the case on many warm days, we ended up in the pool.

Our granddaughter is only about 5 months old, so what do you think the first thing her mother did when it was time to get into the water?

You guessed it, she protected her. How? By surrounding her with an inflatable tube that held her nice and tight and then Mom also stayed right next to her holding onto the tube.

She wanted to make sure that her baby girl was safe and to be close enough to help her if by chance she began to topple over.

On the other end of the pool was our 14-year-old daughter. She was swimming around without any tube or inflatable. She was jumping off the diving board, swimming to the bottom of the deep end of the pool, and essentially had no protection around her.

Saving and investing are as different as our granddaughter and our daughter in the swimming pool.

When we save we have protection, safety, and in some cases, we even have someone there to hold onto us in case of financial problems - we have guarantees.

Like our granddaughter in the tube, she was in the pool and having fun, but was protected, safe, and had someone there to help her if she needed it.

Our daughter on the other hand was unprotected, in the deep end and could, if not careful, find herself in trouble.

Like swimming in the deep end without protection, investing requires that you take a risk. Even though it may be fun, and can be fun, we have no protection. We are at risk. We can run into trouble, and even drown if we aren't careful.

My point is that there is a significant difference between *saving* and *investing*.

Saving typically means your money is going to be there for you – safe, protected.

You don't have to worry so much about the

dangers and pitfalls. Whereas investing requires you to accept the risk of loss if the markets should change along with the dangers associated with the investment.

Sadly, many people think they are *saving* inside of a 401(k), but when you look at the underlying assets, typically mutual funds, they are in fact *investing and even speculating.*

They have no guarantees nor do they understand what is really going on with the investment and the outcome of course is unknown.

We all know someone (maybe even ourselves) that has lost money in an investment of some sort. It could be stocks, real estate, or a 401(k).

Are you aware of the risk you are taking, and can accept the risks and ultimately can live with the risk of loss?

After living through the growth years of the eighties and nineties, I think many of us have a warped sense of what risk really is. 2007-2009 have perhaps awakened many of us into what risk really is!

Yet we still see people funding their 401(k)'s, IRA's, and mutual funds with what they perceive as *savings dollars* into accounts that are essentially speculative investments.

When we talk about creating your own banking system, we are talking about *SAVING* **not** investing or speculating.

This money that goes into your account needs to be safe, liquid, and even have a guarantee associated with it. It has all the necessary ingredients to let us save our money safely and so that it is there for us when we need it, or if our families need it... even at death.

The Long Life

Hopefully a long life is in your future. This is the assumption most of our clients would like us to make, and quite frankly the most difficult of the two "lives."

There is a way to provide for those short-term needs if an unexpected and early death occurs, plus it's simple and inexpensive.

There isn't anything wrong with creating a banking system, but if there isn't enough death benefit in the beginning of the process, add a small term rider to the policy. It will not only make provision in case of a tragedy, but it will also be convertible into permanent life if/when funds are available to create an even larger bank for your family to use. It's a win, win situation.

If you live a long life, you need to prepare for some sort of retirement. This means you need to save or invest.

In the meantime, you have all these pesky expenses that come up which take away your income.

You may also want to enjoy some of the things this world can give you such as cars, boats, second homes, vacations, and so forth. You can finance these items or pay cash. Or you could choose the third option of being your own banker.

Most weeks you will find me sitting down with couples and looking over their finances. I've seen it a thousand times. It seems the same situation presents itself time and time again. What I find is typical in most family's budgets: A breakdown of the after-tax income which goes something like this:

Where Money Goes After Taxes

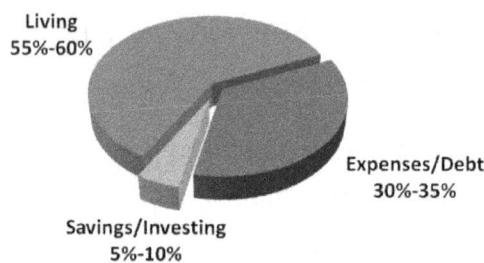

Living
55%-60%

Expenses/Debt
30%-35%

Savings/Investing
5%-10%

I want you to see something that might shock you at first and then the light will go on and you'll say, "Duh, why didn't I think of that?"

Here we have typical Mr. and Mrs. American, we'll call them Fred and Wilma, and they are trying to create a future nest egg to supplement their future income needs with 5%-10% of their net income. Let's forget about the 60% living expenses for now and assume we can't do a thing about that, even though we probably could over time.

We can even assume that they may have taken as much as 6%-8% of their pre-tax income and put it into some sort of retirement plan. But again, let's forget about that for now.

Once you see the overall picture here, you will understand why families are encouraged and even "forced" to take so much risk with their savings and investment dollars. For this example, I'm going to use 5% of their income dedicated to saving/investing.

Look at what the 5% savings has to do for them. The 5% savings has to get such an outlandish and unattainable rate of return, just to keep them above water. Why?

This is due to the fact that the 5% savings has to compensate for the 35% of their income which is wasted by being diverted for debt purposes. It is unnecessary if they understand banking.

If Fred and Wilma could have even a portion of the 35% that is currently going to banks come back to them, it would have a much greater impact on their wealth than the rate of return on their 5% savings.

If they were making $75,000 a year, and had 35% of their income going towards debt, that is $26,250 a year.

If they were saving even 10% each year, that is $7500.

Suppose they got 10% return on their investments.

That's $750 a year.

Yet over $26,000 is being lost or given away to other banks.

All they would need to do is be the financial institution for a portion of what's going out and they would increase their wealth much faster than the 10% rate of return on their savings.

If they were the financing institution of 10% of what is currently being lost – that is $2600.

At 20% they have $5200 coming back to them each year.

The objective of course is to have the majority of your financing needs being controlled by you.

Why an Insurance Company?

This is a question that I'm often asked when determining the best vehicle for a banking system.

It's a great question. It is quite honestly one of the first things I asked as well. There are several other options for a banking system. Here are few of them:

- Checking account
- Savings Account
- Money Market

- Mutual Funds

However, none of them give you the same benefits as a dividend-paying permanent life insurance policy.

First thing we can do is eliminate the mutual fund as a possible alternative. For one, we do not want to risk our capital.

When we want or need a loan, we do not want to have to worry about market timing and hope our money is still worth what we invested. What's worse is, if we take a loan from a mutual fund and the value has dropped significantly, what then? We could end up with less than what we originally invested.

Not only are our premiums guaranteed within an insurance company, but so is a minimum interest rate.

Most insurance companies outperform their guaranteed rate. However, it is nice to know that if things got really bad, that you will at least have a minimum guaranteed rate of return. Keep in mind that the interest rate is really meaningless if we take full advantage of the banking system.

Looking at all the options above or any other

option other than insurance, there is another downfall that all of them have in common.

They are all taxable. Every year, whether you use the money or not, you are sent a 1099 requiring you to claim the interest, dividend, or capital gain income for the year. As previously discussed, this has a major impact on the growth of the account.

Within an insurance policy, all the income is growing tax deferred. You do not get a 1099 for the income earned each year.

Furthermore, if we handle the funds properly, we may never be taxed on the policy values again. Think about it, having money in an account where it may never be taxed again can be a very significant financial gain!

Dividends

Mutual whole life companies pay what is called a dividend. To put this very simply, a dividend in reality is considered to be a *return of premium*.

Let me give you an example.

Suppose we have a premium of $1,000 per year. The insurance company arrived at that number by going through their actuarial calculations – i.e. a process to determine, statistically, how many people and at what age, are going to die this year.

With all the mortality data available to insurance companies, they have become very skillful and adept at pinpointing the number of death claims in a given year.

They don't know when YOU specifically are going to die, but they can tell you how many men or women your age will die this year – within a margin of error.

In our example - let's make this really simple. Out of the $1,000 that the insurance company takes in premium, they have to account for the following:

- Management - Employees
- Offices/Buildings
- Investments/Cash Value – for You
- Death Benefit

A wise insurance company will take more in premium then it expects to pay out in death benefits.

Not only are they required to have excess capital available (Capital Reserve Requirement), but it is smart business as well.

At the end of the year, let's assume the insurance company was correct on their death benefit assumptions, they lived within their budget for expenses, and managed the excess cash conservatively as well.

The insurance company then calculates all of the "expenses" and realizes it has leftover money. In other words - excess premium. What the insurance company projected would cost $1,000 to cover only cost $910.

This leaves the insurance company $90 that can be returned to the policy owner as a "dividend." A return of premium.

Because the initial premium – in our case the $1,000 – was after tax income, the return of premium or dividend is NOT taxable.

Once again if the insurance company is conservative they will keep some of the $90 in reserve and send the remaining amount to each policy owner in the form of a policy dividend.

The dividend can be used to purchase more insurance, commonly referred to as PAID UP ADDITIONS, or reinvested into cash value, or taken directly as additional income.

Dividends for many companies have been paid for over 100+ years - consistently.

Now, here is the best part. For most mutual insurance companies, the dividend is paid even if you have a loan outstanding.

So, your money grows and compounds even if you took a loan.

Paid Up Additions

"Paid up additions" (PUA) is an extremely important component not only to a whole life policy, but to the banking system as well.

For now, let's discuss what a PUA actually is. At its very essence, it is fully paid for insurance.

Each premium payment into a well-designed whole life policy would be split into the "base premium" and the "PUA."

The base premium is the cost to keep the policy alive. This money goes to the cost of insurance and also increases cash value.

Suppose you are 25 years old and in good health. From the insurance company's perspective if you purchase a one-year term policy, the insurance company is only obligated to pay out a death benefit if you died that year.

That is probably a very safe risk. The insurance company would likely bet that you won't die and thus would cover you for a one-year term policy very inexpensively.

Statistically speaking, the insurance company is going to win this bet. As I said previously, only about 1% - 2% of all the term insurance bought ever pays out a death benefit.

However, if they are going to cover you for your entire life, they would have to receive a larger premium for the risk taken.

It is similar to a time value of money calculation.

Let's suppose an insurance company contracted to cover your death for $100,000 during your entire life.

The company would have to know the probability of your death and at what age. I don't know what the answer is, but let's say it's 78 years old.

The insurance company will then need to calculate how much money they need today in premium in order to invest it and make sure they have the

$100,000 to pay out at death at age 78.

They expect to pay it. As you can imagine that might be a complicated calculation. But insurance companies are very good at this calculation. The brains behind these calculations are called "Actuaries. "

Paid up additions are unique to whole life policies. They allow the insured to buy more death benefit without opening a new policy or proving insurability.

Previously when discussing dividends, we said that dividends are paid on death benefit. Think of the insurance policy like buying a stock.

By the way, the term "dividends" came from insurance companies and adopted by Wall Street.

The death benefit is similar to the number of shares of stock that I own.

The dividend in a stock company is paid out on a per share basis. So, the more shares I have the larger the dividend will be.

Then I reinvest the dividend and it buys me more shares of stock.

This repeats itself year after year. I accumulate

more shares of stock each year and my dividend subsequently gets larger and larger.

In a whole life policy, the death benefit is like the "shares of stock."

The dividend is paid out on a per share basis (death benefit).

The dividend is used to buy PUA's, or more shares – which equals more death benefit.

The death benefit increases each year with the reinvested PUA's.

The dividend increases because I have more death benefit (shares).

Once PUA is purchased, there is no longer a cost of insurance for that amount of death benefit. It is FULLY PAID UP.

Side note: This is a HUGE and IMPORTANT concept. A whole life policy is the only policy that you OWN the death benefit. It can be paid up. You can never own the insurance in term policy or a universal life. You are always renting death benefit in those types of policies and the rent gets more expensive each year.

In the end, the larger my death benefit, the greater

my dividend. And as a reminder, dividends are income tax free.

One powerful use of this type of concept is to supplement retirement income from the dividends.

This can be a tax-free additional income stream or even your main source for income during retirement.

Although dividends are not guaranteed to be paid out each year, as mentioned many companies have been paying dividends for 100 to 150 years or more. They are good at what they do.

A banking policy will incorporate a decent sized Paid Up Additions Rider.

This will create almost instant cash value as well. Each year the PUA is funded, the policy will continue to increase the death benefit, but more importantly, additional cash value will be available for banking purposes.

The side benefit is the increasing death benefit. This is extremely important in keeping up with inflation or purchasing power.

Let's suppose we buy a $500,000 policy today and the death benefit remains constant. What happens to the purchasing power of that $500,000 thirty years from now due to inflation? Put another way, will $500,000 buy today what it could have bought back in 1980? Absolutely not!

Whole life has a built-in mechanism to continually increase the death benefit through PUAs. This will be a wonderful benefit to your family. It will protect them from a significant loss of purchasing power years from now while increasing a tax-free dividend as well.

I hope you are catching on that a properly designed and funded whole life policy has so many side benefits in additional to acting more like a bank than a traditionally designed insurance policy.

What's more, this type of policy has been around for as long as 200 years, but few take full advantage of its widespread benefits.

The financial world has become so complex and so complicated it's nearly impossible to decide who to believe or what products to invest in.

Advisors lure you in with talk of high rates of return, when in reality they can rarely, if ever, achieve them – at least on consistently.

Remember, when you chase high rates of return,

who's at risk, the advisor making the recommendation or YOU?

Understanding and controlling "financing" or "banking" is much more important and will have a much greater impact on your wealth than rate of return.

The typical financial planning community has it all wrong.

The Final Benefit

What is the final benefit? It is the lump sum of money that is paid out at the death of the insured – The Death Benefit.

If a policy is designed more for cash value than for death benefit, a wonderful thing happens. Not only is the policy's cash value growing while you are living. But in the tragic event of the insured's death, an instant estate is created and a legacy of the banking system lives on.

This is no small benefit.

Remember when we discussed the need to prepare for two lives? One you live a long and prosperous life and die at an old age. And in the other, you tragically die young.

A properly designed banking system can accommodate both lives. While living, your wealth will naturally grow by using the banking system for all your purchases. But, if by chance death comes early, the wealth that you would have created over your lifetime will be instantly created and your family will have the necessary means to financially survive. It truly is a win-win process.

Many families and business are using high cash value life insurance for many of their financial needs.

Having a strategy to implement and build an engineered policy could also provide the predictability and stability you are looking for as well.

It's worth exploring!

Real Life

You may be asking yourself, who else uses life insurance as a mean to build wealth?

Let me give you some real-life examples.

Walt Disney:

Walt was a very savvy individual, known for his success in business and finance, and had been stockpiling cash into his life insurance policies. Since banks and lenders continued to reject his financing needs, he decided to provide his own financing.

Among other things, Walt borrowed against his cash value life insurance policies, and in 1955, Disneyland opened its doors for the first time. Within 1 year over 3.5 million people visited the park. It was an instant success.

Ray Kroc – McDonalds:

You may have seen the movie "Founder" recently, which doesn't paint Ray Kroc in the greatest light, but no one can argue that he built the McDonald's franchise to a massive company.

Ray didn't take a salary for 8 years. He made good use of his two cash value life insurance policies to help overcome constant cash-flow problems.

He used them to help cover the salaries of key

employees, to pay for unforeseen expenses, and he even used some of the money to create an advertising campaign around the infamous Ronald McDonald Today, McDonald's serves more than 50 million people every day, with more than 30,000 locations around the world. Much of the success of McDonald's can be attributed to Ray's wise use of cash value life insurance.

Pampered Chef:

Doris Christopher believed women needed tools to help them make cooking quicker and easier.

Using her cash value life insurance policy, Doris funded the first inventory for what is now a billion-dollar company with over 12 million customers.

JC Penney:

When the market crashed in 1929, JC Penney, then a dry goods store for mining and farm families, was severely affected.

As the sole owner, James Cash Penney took a huge dive in company and personal wealth. The financial setbacks were so devastating that it even took a toll on his physical and mental health.

Fortunately, Mr. Penney had accumulated massive wealth inside his cash value life insurance policies, and was able to borrow against them to help the company stay afloat and eventually rebound. If he hadn't used cash value life insurance

as a tool to keep his money safe and accessible, it likely wouldn't have been there, and JC Penney would have likely closed its doors.

When he died, the Grand Rapids Press wrote the following about him: "In the Great Stock Market Crash of 1929 he was almost wiped out, but with the money he borrowed on his $3 million-dollar life insurance policy, he was able to rebound."

Today, JC Penney takes in revenues of $18 billion a year and has over 1,100 stores worldwide.

There are literally millions more from every walk of life in every area of the country.

The cash values of life policies have become a staple and a foundational asset for wealth.

Other Strategies

We have been discussing the banking process - a way to create and maintain wealth for both families and businesses.

It's important to understand that one size does not fit all. It takes some planning to determine not only if the banking system is a good fit for you based on age, health, family objectives, and so forth, but if there are other strategies that may be effective for your situation as well.

This book was written to open the discussion on the banking process.

However, we implement many different strategies based on our client's personal needs.

Some of the other strategies we utilize are:

Generating Income – with greater tax benefits

- Gifting – to charities/non-profits – without disinheriting the family
- Gifting – for several generations
- Protecting a disabled or handicapped family member
- Using Arbitrage to increase income and protect your estate

- Reducing/Eliminating estate taxes
- Alternatives to "Reverse Mortgages"
- Stretch or multi-generational IRA's
- Using equity from your home
- Business continuity and protection – including buy/sell – key man – and banking
- Leveraged Retirement
- Asset protection and income deductions for business owners
- Protecting your estate from lawsuits
- Family Split Dollar Trusts
- Several other strategies…..

Each one of these strategies could become another volume in and of itself (and some day may be). These ideas and concepts are simple, effective, and easy to implement.

However, it requires an expert beyond the "traditional" financial planner. This is "out of the box thinking." You want a "financial-prenuer."

No longer can you blindly put money into a retirement plan, pick and choose about any mutual fund, or rely upon the stock market to create the wealth you will need.

Sadly, most advisors have no concept or even

realize that these strategies exist. They are lackeys for the financial industry still peddling the same old concepts, that DO NOT WORK!

When discussing our strategies with clients, the light goes on and I often hear, "Where have you been for the last 20 years and why hasn't anyone told me these strategies even exist?" We take pride in using techniques and ideas that are not common

The Banking Process being one of them.

What's Next?

Will you be the next millionaire or billionaire to use their cash value as a stepping stone towards wealth? Who knows? But one thing is certain, you can get out of the traffic of Wall Street and walk with the wealthy – on the sidewalk - while building and reaching your goal of becoming financially free too.

Warren Buffet has said, that when it's raining gold you want to go out with a wash-tub, not a thimble, and get all the gold you can.

The only way to take advantage when it's raining gold is to have capital.

Capital is KING.

Those with the money when the opportunities come along, get the gold!

When you can buy $10-dollar bills for $5, you'd better get all they will sell you.

The banking system lets you store your capital, be patient, and then get the wash tub out when the gold starts to fall from the sky!

But it all starts with building a capital account in

your own private banking system.

I welcome any questions you may have; my contact info is below.

 It's worth exploring to see if this concept fits into your situation and helps get to the goal of wealth.

Take care!

Biography

Dan Thompson

Wise Money Tools, LLC

208-939-5910

Email: danthompsonsdesk@gmail.com

Dan is the founder of Eagle Capital Management and Wise Money Tools.

Dan has received national recognition for his work in innovative financial strategies.

Dan began licensing as a Financial Advisor in 1986.

Dan originates from Central California where he watched many of his mentors attain wealth by hard work, proper money management, and conservative approaches to investing.

Dan and his wife, Sharon, are the parents of 5 children, and 10 grandchildren.

Dan still enjoys playing basketball and is also on the promo water-ski team for Ski Nautique Ski Boats.